THE WEATHER FACTORY

THE WEATHER FACTORY
A Pictorial History
of Medicine Hat

David C. Jones
L. J. Roy Wilson
Donny White

Western Producer Prairie Books
Saskatoon, Saskatchewan

Cover photographs courtesy Medicine Hat Museum and Art Gallery Archives; photograph bottom right courtesy Glenbow Archives

Cover and book design by John Luckhurst/GDL
Quotations on pages 21 and 22 reprinted with permission from *Time* magazine

Printed and bound in Canada

The publisher wishes to acknowledge the support received for this publication from the Canada Council.

Western Producer Prairie Books is a unique publishing venture located in the middle of western Canada and owned by a group of prairie farmers who are members of Saskatchewan Wheat Pool. From the first book in 1954, a reprint of a serial originally carried in the weekly newspaper *The Western Producer,* to the book before you now, the tradition of providing enjoyable and informative reading for all Canadians is continued.

Canadian Cataloguing in Publication Data

Jones, David C., 1943–

The weather factory: a pictorial history of Medicine Hat

(The City series)
ISBN 0–88833–247–5

1. Medicine Hat (Alta.) – History – Pictorial works.
2. Medicine Hat (Alta.) – Description – Views.
I. Wilson, LeRoy John, 1937– II. White, Donny, 1953–
III. Title. IV. Series.

FC3699.M4J65 1988   971.23′4   C88–098027–3
F1079.5.M4J65 1988

58,814

To Eva Davison, Hope Hargrave Michael, and others,
for their commitment to the archives of the early
Medicine Hat Museum

Acknowledgements

For broadening our understanding of the past, the authors thank the late Jaque Duggan, Don Lefever, Malcolm Sissons, Roy Keating, Cliff Wright, Betty Butler, Frank Anderson, Manuel Raber, Wally Hayne, Jim Turner, Jim McCorkle, and Jim Hirsch. We are also grateful to Jim Simpson, Tom Willock, and Frank Webber who reproduced the photographs from the Medicine Hat Archives and to Kathy Dirk who was research assistant. For help with city records and development, we note Larry Godin and David Cormier; with Monarch Broadcasting and the CHAT Television photograph collection, Bill Yuill, Barbara Ayling, and Loreen Piehl-Wiedemann; and with the *Medicine Hat News* photographs, Peter Mossey. For facilitating the use of the Hat Archives, we thank the Medicine Hat Museum and Art Gallery Trustees. For direction and technical aid we acknowledge archivists and librarians Doug Cass, Kathryn Myhr, Lindsay Moir, Lynette Walton, and Merrily Aubrey, as well as cartographer Marta Styk. For funding the work we salute the University of Calgary Grants Committee, the Medicine Hat College Research Committee, and the Alberta Foundation for the Literary Arts.

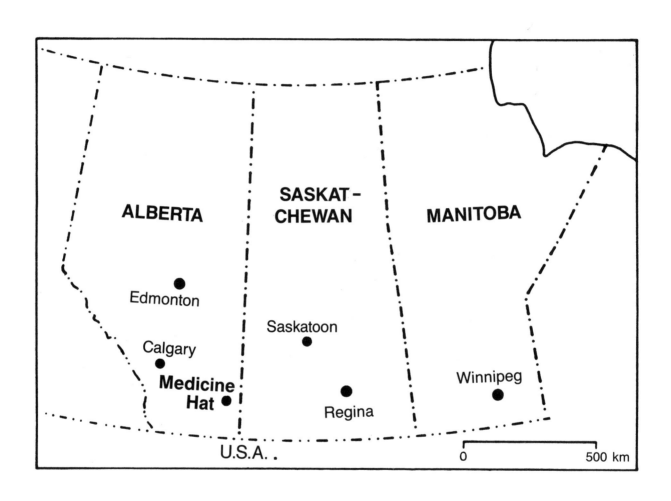

ALBERTA

SASKAT-
CHEWAN

MANITOBA

Edmonton

Calgary

**Medicine
Hat**

Saskatoon

Regina

Winnipeg

U.S.A.

0   500 km

Introduction

BEGINNINGS
"The Place Will Soon Be Overdone"

Medicine Hat: A station on the main line of the C.P.R., 660 miles west of Winnipeg; has telegraph and express offices. Mail daily. Pop. about 500. Stage leaves for Fort Macleod every Monday morning; leaves Fort Macleod for Medicine Hat, connecting with C.P.R. express going east, every Sunday morning.
Henderson's North West Gazetteer and Directory, *1884*

Surveyors must have been impressed when they discovered the valley. At the confluence of three water systems was a luxuriant oasis, nestled amid the endless stretch of prairie desert. In this great valley the mingling and confrontation of ancient tribes occurred, and legends grew, several explaining the origin of the fascinating name, "Medicine Hat." Was it not here that the Blackfoot leader lost his war bonnet? Or was it that the Medicine Man saw his headdress reflected in the quiet river water, took it as an omen of victory against his enemies, and thereafter endowed the spot "Miskeke Estowtin," the place of the Medicine Hat? Perhaps the name came from the slaughter of a party of white settlers and the theft of a frilled hat from one of the victims. Or from the shape of a nearby hill, or of the townsite itself which resembled an inverted medicine bonnet. Or maybe James Sanderson was right. The renowned half-breed scout and trader was well acquainted with the valley. Below the cliffs where the ice never freezes, he recounted, dwelt a serpent which could communicate with man. The serpent received the sacrifice of an Indian warrior's sweetheart, and directed the brave to the hiding place of the charmed hat which made him the mightiest of Cree chiefs. Whatever story one fancies—and there were more—to the ancient people the place was special.

At the "place of the Medicine Hat" the railway bridge would be built. Knowing the track was coming, a motley band of youthful squatters gathered in the valley in fall 1882. The large Edward McKay half-breed clan was there, discharged Mounties like Robert McCutcheon, Fred Mountain, and Bill Johnston, former fur-trade boys and their Indian wives, and any number of vagabonds. Opportunists all, they wanted first crack at the new frontier.

Early next June immense grading crews moved down Ross Creek to Seven Persons Coulee and built the roadbed, with difficulty, to the river. Instantly, a city of tents mushroomed, with hotels, general stores, and barbershops catering to the crowds of big spenders. So furious was the influx and the makeshift assemblage that the travelling Toronto *Globe* correspondent reported on June 10: "If they continue to pour in the way they have yesterday and today, the place will soon be overdone!"

Construction of the twelve-hundred-foot wooden bridge, the rough railway buildings, and the track yards stimulated more work. With thousands of men enriching the saloonkeepers in their off-hours, the North-West Mounted Police wisely posted a large detachment on the rim of the valley across the river. There, at Police Point, a substantial barracks temporarily housed a squadron of officers and men.

Speedily the entrepôt developed. At first a weekly stagecoach ran to Fort Macleod, and by 1884 steamboats plied between Coalbanks (later Lethbridge) and the Hat. Next summer the dominion government erected a large immigrants' hall which doubled as a community entertainment centre for years. Frame structures replaced tents, and when the Corbin brickyard began production in 1886, an air of permanency materialized.

Soon a fascinating array of human migrants of every colour and contour gathered—German farmers from the Cypress Hills buying and selling, American traders turning the place upside-down every Fourth of July, and Chinese restaurateurs and laundrymen, butt of so much racist slander. Remarkable characters appeared—Vincent Minneszewsky, the Polish count with the reputation for a hair-trigger temper; barber Bill Adams, sot and wife beater; "Dublin" O'Brien, half-wit, who spent most winters in the Maple Creek jail, a guest of the government. The most notorious bootlegger was vulgar Annie Moran, and the self-styled first "white" woman in the region was "Nigger" Mollie Smith. No stranger to police cells, she too regularly applied firewater to local Indians. From the beginning the town had its plague of prostitutes as well.

Usually simmering in some dingy cathouse at town edge, the harlots flaunted themselves openly on the streets, baiting the boys already stirred by the sparcity of females on the frontier.

Gradually social affairs expanded beyond the sirens. Travelling artists like Pauline Johnson, the Mohawk poetess, came to the Opera House; the Georgia Minstrels, the Dixie Jubilee singers, and the "Coontown 400" sang the songs of the Old South; celebrants picnicked at Strathcona Island or Police Point, or took evening paddle-wheeler excursions to Galt Island. Sports proliferated and included the local 1886 Territorial cricket champions; a baseball club prepared to take all comers for "fun, money or marbles"; a lacrosse club so rough it once knocked five men out in a single scrimmage; J. C. Colter's gas-lit indoor skating rink; and ferryman W. R. Johnston's famous floating "swimming baths" on the river.

There were bicycle, tennis, gun, curling, snowshoeing, and horse racing clubs. In 1899 a golf club sat on the hilltop south of Toronto Street School. Even ladies' hockey was played, though in the nineties, at least, no one was permitted to witness it. The reason was apparently revealed later when the door was left ajar and a nasty reporter viewed the clash of the Titans, the "Bachelor Girls" versus the "Sisters-in-bondage." "The members of the two teams looked very neat as they lined up in their natty golf sweaters and their chic little toques," he wrote tongue-in-cheek. In the fury of battle while Miss Gilbert fainted repeatedly from a rude body check, the others "spent a large portion of their time straightening their hats and keeping their skirts hanging properly." The rink, he hinted plainly, was a powder room in disguise.

Such levity helped mask the harsher realities of town life—the grime and the grit, for example. The laundryman or "washee washee" slopped his dirty water into the thoroughfares where it mixed with "loathsome, foul-smelling accumulations of filth" like bones, decaying vegetables, ashes, old boots, and cans dumped by others. Every spring, complained the Hat *News*, the refuse turned the town into a "hottentot kraal."

Prairie fires added smoke, and the winds, dust. "The wind dust blow," moaned the paper. So drab was the overall portrait that it justified J. G. Donkin's comment in *Trooper and Redskin* (1889) that a prairie town was "a more depressing object than a burnt forest."

The irritating aura seemed to overspill social affairs, widening all the natural cleavages between Catholics and Orangemen, liquor men and temperance men, businessmen and railroaders. For a decade beginning in the late 1880s, wrangling reigned supreme, centring on the enigmatic local railway mogul John Niblock. An Ontarian, he arrived in Medicine Hat in 1887. A benefactor and humanitarian to his friends, he was to his enemies an ogre and autocrat.

Niblock knew trees. He had at one time in Ontario been in the tree business, the kind that grew fruit as well as the ones required for windbreaks and decoration. His was an object lesson as to what could be done in a new country. He had one crabapple tree that was a great joke to his higher-ups. On one occasion when Mr. Van Horne and friends came over the road J.N. took them in charge at Swift Current. Van Horne's first salutation was, "Hello, John, how is the crabapple tree?" J.N. replied, "It's fine, sir. When we get to the 'Hat I will show you a good crop of crabapples and you can have some for your supper if you like that kind of fruit." Van laughed and said, "You are going bughouse John. You have no apples on trees in these Territories, unless you tied them on." Someone in authority wired the 'Hat to have all the crabapples pulled off the tree, and when the town was reached Mr. Van Horne said, "Come on John, show us your apples." There were none to be seen, of course. There was a big laugh. Was John mad— make your own guess. He was guilty of getting mad occasionally.
William Cousins, The Lethbridge Herald, *March 29, 1938*

Teetotaler, Orangeman, rigid Methodist, and rumoured member of the extremist Protestant Protective Association, Niblock stood with the Sons of Temperance and the Royal Templars of Temperance in cursing liquor and gambling. Since the Hat was infamous for gaming and boozing (despite Territorial prohibition till 1892), not all appreciated him. Undeterred, he chastised employees who gambled on their own time or who patronized local tipplers, and he was accused of discriminating against Catholics in hiring and against unfriendly railway customers in business. His chief nemesis, J. D. Drinnan of *The Times*, charged: "It is about time Mr. Niblock was told, in unmeasured terms, he does not own the bodies and souls of the free and independent citizens of Medicine Hat and he cannot with impunity smirch their characters."

Drinnan, former schoolmaster, attacked Niblock's pride and joy, the new hospital, for favouritism in purchasing procedures. Then he accused local Roadmaster James Horner of attempting to rape a "poor defenseless foreign girl," and demanded an inquiry. When the girl and her family withdrew the charge, however, Horner sued *him*, forcing him to apologize publicly.

Fed up, Niblock and allies withdrew advertising from *The Times* and plotted Drinnan's retirement. Amid rumours of a rival news rag in early 1894, Drinnan defiantly exclaimed, "The Times is here to stay." A month later, in depression, economic and emotional, he sold out to the Medicine Hat News Company, the shareholders of which were all supporters of John Niblock.

That summer Drinnan helped form the Medicine Hat Citizens' Committee. It comprised William Cousins, a town father, James Hargrave, merchant and rancher, Dr. J. G. Calder, many ranchers, and others. Forthwith it petitioned the CPR to remove Niblock.

Simultaneously, William Finlay, another town father, circulated a counter petition signed by Thomas Tweed, MLA, numerous farmers, ranchers, merchants, and railway-men. "We, your petitioners," it stated, "consider Mr. Niblock as our best citizen and friend and feel that he is being hounded and persecuted by an unprincipled clique, humbly beg that no action will be taken." Impressed, the railway did nothing.

That October the feud continued in the Territorial elections. Frustrated, the Drinnan–Cousins forces supported Maple Creek rancher Edward L. Fearon over incumbent Thomas Tweed, a prime beneficiary of hospital contracts. When Fearon won, Cousins and cronies ignited a huge bonfire on the prairie in celebration, capped later by a parade and banquet. In the ensuing school board elections, the ritual was reversed. The Niblock–Tweed faction won, and only a feast silenced the resounding hosannas.

The feud lasted till December 1898. Then, at a memorable hospital Thanksgiving supper, William Cousins extended the hand of peace. To hushed listeners he said, "The scrap is over."

The next year Niblock was transferred. He left a legacy of turmoil, a $20,000 hospital, first in the Territories, and the magnificent CPR gardens—models, he believed, of what man could do on the Prairies.

To visitor Rudyard Kipling, however, even the gardens were disturbing. The beautifully laid out flower plots, the lawn, the shrubs, and the fruit trees nursed so lovingly were incongruous against the backdrop of the wooden town and the raw prairie.

It was an insight forgotten as the settlement of the Canadian West gathered pace.

BOOM
"Calgary is Nowhere"

Where land is producing from 30 to 60 bushels of the best grade wheat in the world; oats yielding 125 bushels to the acre and weighing out 45 to 50 lbs to the bushel; flax yielding 18 to 25 bushels to the acre; barley yielding 60 bushels to the acre as plump and bright as ever grew; rye as tall as your head, producing two crops a year; alfalfa, peerless in quality and in great quantity, root crops of all kinds in abundance, small fruits of all kinds, and where the land is just being developed and still remains very cheap in price, surely such a land is worthy of investigation.

F. M. Ginther, We Sell the Earth, 1913

After a disastrous fire pointed to the advantages of civic organization, Medicine Hat was consecrated as a town in 1898. By century-end, Hatters had become cautiously optimistic. A rejuvenated board of trade and a new courthouse were established in 1900, and plans for expansion of boundaries, gas lines, water-works, and sidewalks were made. Tillers were even enjoying a rainy cycle, and shortly after 1901 the population doubled to 3,000.

Unhappily the growth was unsustained. Board-of-traders soon became impatient with the lack of public dedication to community welfare and with the overlap between city council's "new enterprises" committee and their own organization. When new industries did not flock in and the seasons turned dry again in 1903, some despaired.

Remember, too, that public spirit means a personal interest felt by every citizen in Medicine Hat . . . a careful, impartial and intelligent study of public affairs; an earnest effort by every voter to secure the best men obtainable to manage the town's business . . . a readiness on the part of every resident to spend time and labor and money to help the town; a municipal loyalty that will make everyone support Medicine Hat people and Medicine Hat institutions, a local patriotism that rises above self, disregarding the little circles in which we move, and seeking nothing but the common good. With this spirit Medicine Hat will prosper.

William Cousins, Board of Trade, Annual Report, *February 15, 1906*

As other parts of the West tore ahead, the Hat lay in irons, waiting for the wind to catch its sails. The town was not ready for the spotlight, for the Dominion had not yet opened its tributary lands for homesteading, and its gas wells were too wet and anemic to attract industry. Even the way of life was dreadfully unurban and unbefitting a place destined for glory.

By 1907 Medicine Hat was still little more than a cowtown in the boondocks. Two out of three houses had barns, and every morning cattle were herded down the streets and sidewalks to the prairie where they munched till dusk before being herded home. Citizens gave right-of-way to the beasts who reciprocated by fertilizing the walks, the streets, the lanes—everything in sight. The town reeked of a feedlot.

The gas bonanza helped change all this. For decades it had been known that swamp gas (methane) underlay the region, but it was deemed more a nuisance than a blessing. In 1883 the CPR went looking for water at Langevin and discovered gas; eight years later it loaned Medicine Hat a drilling outfit to seek coal and found more gas. Poorly pressurized, the gas was also damp and had to be dried before use, a costly process.

The city determined to drill deeper in 1904, hoping for a drier, fuller flow. Down the bit bore 950 feet, bringing nothing but consternation and cost. The allocation spent and people grumbling, the city council huddled in secret at night. Desperately, it heard the driller's plea for more time, and finally, exceeding his powers, Mayor Hutchinson granted the request. The next morning, at 1,010 feet, the well blew in, expelling 600 pounds of pressure per square inch of whistle-dry methane. Industrial Medicine Hat was born.

Seven deep wells supplied the city by early 1913, yielding four million cubic feet a day at dirt cheap prices. While rates in other Canadian cities ranged from $1.00 to $1.75 per thousand cubic feet, in the Hat they were 13½ cents for homes and a nickel for industries. The doors of an eight-room house could be propped open permanently, and still the heat bill wouldn't reach fifty dollars a year. A big hotel burned less than a dollar's worth a day, even in winter. It was cheaper to keep the city's gas lamps burning night and day than to hire a man to turn them on and off.

Rudyard Kipling, poet and tourist of the Empire, said it best when he claimed the area had "all hell for a basement." Surely the Hat was "born lucky." All it needed was a market for the products of its furnace, and manufacturers the world over would come clamouring. When the vast drylands surrounding the Hat were opened to homesteaders in December 1908, the market materialized.

Until a few years ago Medicine Hat was essentially a "cow-puncher's town," being the centre of an enormous ranching district, and it is still one of the largest shipping points of ranch products in the West. The rancher is, however, being fast driven back into the open country, and the ranges that will remain for a number of years will be in the Cypress Hills, to the south-east, and on the Red Deer and Saskatchewan Rivers, to the north-east. The reason for the passing of the range is the enormous influx of new settlers. . . .
Board of Trade, Medicine Hat, Alberta, Canada, 1910

In the first seven months of 1910, 5,138 homesteads, comprising 822,000 acres, were gobbled up. Overnight, new burgs erupted from the flats and were boosted to the skies—Carlstadt, "the star of the prairie," Redcliff, "the smokeless Pittsburgh," Winnifred, "another town born lucky," and Suffield, the prize of the Southern Alberta Land Company, with its future "lake" and "summer resort."

At this sublime moment, the matter of appearances drew attention in the Hat. Some upstarts were frankly embarrassed by the name of the place, reckoning it to be too unwieldy and uncivilized. The *Sporting Times* of London suggested that "Cocked Hat" might be more appropriate.

"Medicine Hat is large-sounding, mouth filling, sonorous, resonant," asserted editor Deighton R. Ware of the re-rooted Hat *Times*. "One feels instinctively that Medicine Hat must be quite a place. It is different from Pincher Creek [also considering a name change] which designation is hopelessly frontier and insignificant." "There is only one Medicine Hat," approved *The Lethbridge Herald;* "there can be only one Medicine Hat; there has been only one Medicine Hat; and there should be a Medicine Hat."

Such sentiments warmed the cockles of Rudyard Kipling's heart. Referring to the old joke, promoted especially by Chicago newsmen, that Medicine Hat was the home of the blizzard because all Territorial storm reports came from its meteorological station, Kipling declared, "Accept the charge joyously and proudly and go forward as Medicine Hat—the only city officially recognized as capable of freezing out the United States and giving the continent cold feet."

An Answer to the Libel on Medicine Hat Weather

> *. . . They say we make the weather*
> *   in a "factory" at the Hat.*
> *And to please their idle fancy*
> *   I will grant them even that;*
> *But there's one thing they've*
> *not noticed, that they may not*
> *   think so fine,*
> *We don't use the kind we're making—*
> *   We just send it 'cross the line.*

Harland E. Fitch

Detailing the advantages of the name Medicine Hat in uniqueness, assertion, and power, Kipling asked finally, "what should a city be rechristened that has sold its name?" He answered—"Judasville."

The Hat name stood trial in December 1910. When the verdict was rendered, it was vindicated by 351 votes to 28.

By that time, the first great industry (save for the flour mill), had arrived. Its plant was enormous and its output prodigious. With eighteen kilns running twenty-one hours a day, the Alberta Clay Products shipped three million bricks to Edmonton and half a million to Saskatoon in 1912, and had orders for hundreds of carloads of hollow tile for Calgary's new Hudson's Bay store and rail facilities. Consuming roughly fifteen million cubic feet of gas annually, the plant was the largest of its kind in Canada and the second largest on the continent.

Following quickly were the Alberta Rolling Mills, the Alberta Foundry and Machine Company, the Alberta Linseed Oil Company, and three more major flour mills. The latter alone cost $2.6 million and employed 475 men. By mid-1914, when the boom was spent, the city produced sixty different articles including brick, building blocks, lime, linseed oil, castings, sewer pipe, pottery, pumps, cylinders, and syrups. Its annual payroll was $2.5 million.

Dishing out concessions by the score—for free sites, free gas or nearly free gas, railway spurs, and exemption from municipal taxation for years—the city expected and got industry after industry. One it missed—and after years of lobbying—the CPR shops. It didn't particularly perturb Hatters that Redcliff claimed *it* was getting the shops (and that soon Medicine Hat would be Redcliff's most important suburb), but in rankled Hatters no end when Calgary got the nod. "Farewell! Oh, thou fond dreams of affluence and sudden glory. Farewell," said Ginger, *The Times* hack. "I weep. The car shops are no more. We loved this young child of our bright hope. We nurtured it. It became a thing of beauty—almost. But the CPR gave and the CPR have taken away! Blessed be the name of the CPR!"

Further down this column of frequent bombast and occasional wit, a fictional newcomer asked, "Where and what is Calgary?"

"Calgary, my dear innocent young friend, is nowhere," came the answer. "It is at present to be located several thousand feet up in the air. It is a name not mentioned in polite circles in this city. It is a creation superinduced by the application to an infinitesimal point of a powerful and continued draft of hot air. A similar result is often witnessed as a phenomenon on these plains in the so-called mirage. Calgary is a myth."

Still fuming a week later, Ginger disgorged the following:

> Oh tell me gentle stranger;
>   Oh tell me, if you please;
> Is Calgary a city?
>   Or is it a disease?

Seldom was Ginger so dyspeptic, so disagreeable. Generally she was glad and giddy and tipsy in the rarefied atmosphere at the pinnacle of prosperity. As she surveyed the metropolis with three liquor stores and six hotels in April 1912, she snorted, "Boozeness must be good." When a cigar factory started, she snapped, "Now watch our smoke!" When the Ogilvie Flour mills announced its coming, she quipped, "The old motto, 'we can and we will,' is changed. Now it is, 'we can and we mill.'"

Reflecting on the passing range, a pity to some, Ginger noted sardonically, "I haven't noticed any of the erstwhile cattle kings watering the prairie with the briny drops over the real estate deals they're making these days." If cattlemen who had lost leases sometimes cried out, their utterances were drowned in the din of wheeling and dealing in the Hat itself.

As the speculative orgy intensified, Ginger remarked, "The old landmarks are fast disappearing (the real estate stakes are crowding out the cacti.)" It was hardly exaggeration.

Real Estate

> *'Twas but a mile or two from here,*
> *I bought a piece of land last year,*
> *   And, why I scarcely knew;*
> *An agent, with a joyful grin,*
> *He jollied me and took me in,*
> *   Until my case came through.*

And ever since I've cursed my lot,
About that bloomin' land I bought.
*   And thought myself a dub.*
My wife wept tears of sorrow, but
She also said I was a mutt,
*   For buyin' in the "Sub."*

I tried to give the stuff away,
The folks around would only say,
*   "Take back your measly gift,*
Pay up the rest, and go and hide
Your head in pickle, till you've died;
*   And give your brains a sift."*

But lo! so many little mills
Are going to settle by our rills,
*   I don't know where I'm at.*
The same old agent bothers me.
To get my lots away from me.
*   By talking through my Hat.*

They compliment me on my brains,
My wife goes out and tells her friends
*   And then she calls me "Dear,"*
My popularity's a joke,
'Twould make a cat sit up and choke
*   To think of me last year.*

anonymous, The Times, March 22, 1912.

By early 1913, of 190 businesses in town, *nineteen* were realties. Druggist Bertram Souch was just closing out his Central Park properties; after five years on the market, they were worth ten times what he paid for them. Rimmer and Smith had recently induced a businessman to buy a quarter-section east of the city; they marketed it, sold it in blocks, and netted their client $11,000. The blocks were then sold as lots, yielding more thousands.

William Cousins too hit the jackpot. Years before, when asked the value of the lands comprising the Cousins–Sisson subdivision, he replied, "Five dollars an acre for pasturage." In 1905 he bought it for twenty dollars an acre, and seven years on, some lots were selling for $5,000 each. In May 1912 his 75-by-130-foot property fronting on Toronto Street and Fourth Avenue sold for $80,000 – a Hat record, over $10,000 a foot!

Through all the madness, the board of trade churned out propaganda by the carload. In 1913 alone it dispensed 40,000 pamphlets and folders, 16,000 copies of the *Medicine Hat Manufacturer*, 10,000 envelope slips, and 200,000 gummed letter seals with a flaming gas well as a centrepiece. It helped provide major publicity pieces for the *Canadian Magazine*, the *Canadian Courier*, the *Traveller's Magazine*, the *World Traveller de Luxe*, *Answers*, and *Canada*, and regular news bulletins for financial journals. Once to thrice a week, it sent special news articles, often illustrated, to all the major cities in Canada and to London, England. In January the board bought a filing cabinet to hold ten thousand letters from the hordes of capitalists seeking entry into what Kipling once called the new "Nineveh." By year-end, the filing cabinet was jam packed.

The city had come of age. It had thirty major industries, twenty-five miles of graded streets, fifty-four miles of waterworks and sewers, eight chartered banks, eight public schools, fourteen churches, four parks, and twenty natural gas wells with a daily flow of fifty million cubic feet. Its population had jumped from 3,020 in 1906 to an estimated 15,000 in 1913.

BUST
"They Were All Easily Humbugged"

Let us not war against this pride of city nor expect to build ourselves up by pulling others down. Let Edmonton boast of her penitentiary, Ponoka her asylum, Red Deer of being the best place for mental defectives in the Dominion, Lethbridge in being a city of refuge for all the criminals of the province, and last, but not least to Calgary belongs the crowning glory of boasting of her slaughterhouse and incidentally the number of hogs one finds running at large through all quarters of the city. Alas, the citizens of Medicine Hat can't compete in a list of honors similar to those which have crowned the labors of the citizens of sister cities in Alberta. . . .

Father O'Mara, Medicine Hat News, *September 14, 1916*

Nothing better symbolized the hopes of the next generation than a ceremony on the plains in fall 1914. Local potentates—including President Laidlaw of the board of trade, Chief Bruce of the police, Mayor Brown of the Hat, and Mayor Bott of Redcliff—mounted eight jalopies and fought through twelve miles of mud and water northwest of the city to a special plot of land. There, before forty wide-eyed witnesses, they turned the first sod on the new Canadian Northern Railroad grade to Hanna. His spade decorated with ribbons and a Union Jack, President Laidlaw dug in and beamed, "This line is another spoke in the wheel of a bigger and greater Medicine Hat."

The crowd cheered, and, urged by Mayor Brown, shouted three hurrahs followed by a tiger for Sir William MacKenzie and the CNR.

Two weeks later the roadbed swarmed with workers. Three camps with over 300 men and 205 teams were going full tilt. "The camps look like little white villages, presaging the towns that will spring up along the line . . . ," *The Times* scribe wrote. They brought their own village blacksmiths, butchers, bakers, and cooks. Stretched over several miles, the graders were speedily bearing down on the Red Deer River.

A stirring spectacle it was, unforgettable and uplifting, but in time, deeply rending and dispiriting, for the line was never completed. No other failure so consumed the Hat Chamber of Commerce for so many decades. Track was laid from Hanna to the river, and the grade, from the river to the Hat. But there it sat forever—90 percent done.

The frustration was only part of the fate of Hatters after 1913. At the height of the 1912–13 boom, Mayor Nelson Spencer forecast the population in a year to be twenty-five to forty thousand. The June census of 1915 was a trifle short at less than nine thousand. By then the city had utilities for four times its population. With three hundred vacant buildings, perhaps four hundred men unemployed, and at year-end, $400 thousand in tax arrears and a whopping $3.7 million debt, retrenchment was the order of the day and depression gripped the land.

The real estate market fell to pieces, room and house rents halved, and the demand for industrial products dissipated. A movement began to stop paying taxes and to let the city go bankrupt.

As Mayor Archie Hawthorne surveyed the industrial core in late 1915, he noted that a dozen major industries—including the Potteries, the Crayon plant, the Tent and Mattress Company, and the Sanitary Fountain Company—were all dead. Further, the Woolen Mills, later the canneries, lay in ruins, and the glass bottle plant was now a stable.

In mid-July a tornado struck Redcliff, demolishing twenty-five buildings. Somehow the Hat was spared, though as if the elements were irked, eight months later the plants of the Dominion Harvester Company and the Lake of the Woods Milling Company were razed by fire. For years after the boom, no one considered either of the twin cities "born lucky."

Deflated, Hatters turned to an old pastime—infighting. Few mayoralty tilts were as fiercely contested as that in 1915. It was the last in which two daily newspapers participated, and with the morning *Times* and the evening *News* bullwhipping each other, it was the best show in town. The first backed former Mayor Nelson Spencer, MP, and the second, the incumbent Archie Hawthorne. Reporting on both sides was the most biased on record.

According to the *News*, Spencer took full credit for the boom, but as for the bust—"Don't blame me, Mr. Taxpayer," he said. The people, after all, voted for all the expenditure. "It was their fault he spent the money. It wasn't his." Spellbound, Spencer had had a vision of a sprawling metropolis; it was sprawling all right, with an extra $2 million millstone around its neck. "The people today are paying the piper for this vision," fumed the paper. "Do Hatters want this dreamer for mayor again?"

Spencer and his ally, another former (and future) mayor, M. A. Brown, had also seized control of the board of trade and were shamelessly using its offices as headquarters in their pursuit of power.

According to *The Times*, "Hidden behind the form of Mayor Hawthorne, are well known citizens—the richest in the community, and most of them engaged in or connected with the liquor business. . . . Make no mistake," it said, "Medicine Hat is being throttled to death by a small ring of moneyed men who control a machine known as the Ratepayers' Association. They don't believe in progress, they don't believe in greater population. They are in favour of selling off property for taxes so they can buy it back again for a song. . . . They made big money out of the city's expansion by sales of property and they have money yet. . . . They want a 'dead game' cinch on the city."

President of the ratepayers' association for 1915 was William Cousins. When Cousins donated thirty-one acres of hillside property to the city, some shouted philanthropy. No so, claimed J. B. Kenrick of *The Times*. The gift with no strings attached really had "fourteen hundred and twenty-five little dollar strings of unpaid taxes!" Recently Cousins had lost his zeal for real estating, having gorged on the windfalls of several subdivision sales. "When these lands were of value, and when the city was in urgent need of land, not a foot could be obtained by the city except at top notch prices," snarled Kenrick. Now they were worth less than the taxes owing on them, and Cousins was "giving" them to the city. Philanthropy? Hardly.

An old realty partner of Cousins, Hawthorne won the election by 808 votes to 545.

As civic discontent brewed on, the war moved centre-stage, relieving the city of its manhood and its unemployed and offering some recompense through munitions and other contracts. The latter, however, were invariably undermined by added freight costs to the front, so the Hat profited little.

Overseas, casualties were so severe that 235 locals were killed—three times the sacrifice of the next conflict. In town, mourners and jingoes hounded and harassed the large German minority, leaving lasting bitterness.

In the countryside, calamity struck. After bumper crops in 1915 and 1916, the first since the land was settled, another briefer bout of wheeling and dealing occurred from 1917–19. Prices then dropped, land values fell, and agriculture began two decades of scarcely interrupted misery. Around the Hat it was bone dry for years.

Hamlets and villages in the dry belt withered, and the empire east of Tilley, between the Red Deer and South Saskatchewan rivers, was utterly depopulated. Around the doomed village of Alderson, thirty-five miles west of the Hat, ten townships alone lost 83 percent of their population in the six years after 1918. Of fifty-two rural schools once in the huge Tilley East region, only eight remained by late 1926.

The disaster constituted the worst farm abandonment in Alberta history—over four times that of the same parts during the Great Depression, and worse by far than anywhere else in Canada at any time.

It was appalling, and in 1928 long-time Medicine Hat pastor Rev. J. W. Morrow said so. When this hinterland filled, it fed the boom; when the Tilley East homesteader became extinct, the Hat languished like a tree with its largest limb dead. Morrow damned the blathering of the Hanna–Hat railroad deputations to the East in the heyday. "Hot air may fool the people of Medicine Hat," he wrote, "—they were always easily humbugged." Just how Sir Henry Thornton of the CNR might be compelled to finish the line when it traversed a vacant desert, recently withdrawn from homesteading and retitled the Tilley East Special Area, baffled the preacher.

The words scored Hat bigwigs who credited themselves more highly and who valued their chances of getting the road more than ever. When they did not thank Morrow, he remarked, "There are always some lepers who do not want their scabs uncovered . . . and [who] probably foresee that . . . I may uncover some wickedness in high places."

There was some evil. The boom had been overdone, and the drylands had been too thickly and too indiscriminately settled. The rest Morrow left implicit—certain locals, real estate agencies, and other boosters had been negligent in marketing a semidesert. They had lied about the fertility of the soil, about farm methods that wrought "wonders," about frost that diminished with each new furrow, about how much rain fell, about how timely it was, and about how unerringly it followed the plough.

The boosting of the empire of dust and its capital had been excessive. Criticism now flowed freely, and knocking, once irredeemable, became almost insightful. Hatters in the twenties coined a new saying: "A few knockers in every town are necessary to keep the boosters from boosting it to death."

Circled by ruin, Medicine Hat stagnated. In 1916 its population was 9,272, and twenty years on, it was 9,592. It would be forty years before the numbers surpassed those of early 1913.

Like a penance, city fathers laboured half a lifetime to rehabilitate the surrounding turf. The interwar period began and ended with irrigation in the spotlight. But nothing happened as outside investment evaporated, project costs skyrocketed, and the senior governments squabbled. With exceptions, irrigation schemes to the mid-1930s in Alberta were colossal failures.

City administration between the wars teetered and almost toppled. After 1918, already debt-ridden, the Hat fell into the financial morass that claimed most cities. For years tax collections totalled only 60 percent of levies, and property was defaulted by the acre. Breathing the heavy air of depression till 1925, the city levied new taxes, and these, combined with higher gas prices, raised local fury.

Medicine Hat was enduring the post-war recession (then called merely "the slump") like the rest of the country. Real estate did not move and the grassy plain beyond the end of 2nd Street was dotted with abandoned frame houses. An enterprising man could pick up a bargain. In one of his walks my father noticed this house, number 417 Allowance Avenue, which was empty, with all windows broken, paint peeling, its interior full of refuse and the yard covered with dead weeds and rubbish. But it was structurally sound and he was a handyman. He made a bid to rent it but the real estate agent refused on the grounds that it was unfit for habitation. My father persisted, offering to renovate it if the owner would pay for materials. Hence for weeks during the spring and early summer he sawed, hammered, painted and puttied while mother and I raked up heaps of refuse and rusted cans. By midsummer we were settled. The house shone with new paint outside and kalsomime inside, vegetables and flowers grew in the garden and we were paying only $5.00 a month rent!

William Temple, Medicine Hat News, June 14, 1971

In the thirties, Medicine Hat agonized over bankruptcy, unprecedented relief charges, assessments that were too high, taxation that was confiscatory. It wondered how it could ever honour bonds coming due for its over-grand utilities and for industrial sites purchased by the city and given away so long ago to so many who were gone. There was talk again that too many manufacturers were running the chamber of commerce and that industries cost more than they were worth.

Amid this sorry state, Hatters turned inward and made the best of times. Cultivating social, literary, and entertainment events by the score, they made the city a cultural centre of uncommon magnitude. In 1922 and 1923, the per capita annual circulation of the public library exceeded that of either Edmonton or Calgary. Almost ten books a year were read by every man, woman, and child in town. Any number of associations flourished—from a philharmonic orchestra, to an operatic society, to dozens of athletic endeavours. By 1935 Medicine Hat was the fourth ranking city in the country in number of Boy Scouts per capita. And there were at least thirty women's organizations in town, excluding the many ladies' auxiliaries and missionary societies.

Despite these activities, the Depression muted the joy of the people and changed their attitudes. More than usual was made of little things, little oddities. Citizens turned the common into the special, savouring the spice of life in its simplest forms.

They had a "tomato war" in 1935, started by Rev. E. J. Church who found a giant Beefeater 12¾ inches around. Mrs. A. Bartoll then showed one an inch bigger, followed by Thomas Shellhorn with three at exactly 15 inches, then fireman Fergus Fraser whose father had reared a red monster with a 17-inch waist.

Once a goose with four wings was the prize attraction at a shopping festival. Another time, someone found a mushroom with a circumference of 41 inches, covering half of Dunmore.

The Depression bred a sardonic sense of humour, a comedy of adversity that accentuated bluntness, outspokenness, and irreverence, and stretched current absurdity to extremes. In an era when progress and triumph had vanished, people found perverse delight in their replacements—in failure and losing.

The year 1939 opened with the *News* report that none other than Nick Schmeling, cousin of former world boxing champion Max, was about to take on Eppie Lust, local pugilist of some repute who had renamed himself, "Young Tunney Lust." At Bow Island in the fifth round, Schmeling took one of the hardest lefts of his career and went down for the count. Unfortunately, the shot was to the groin. "The blow paralyzed one of Schmeling's legs," observed the reporter, "and although his arms were perfectly willing to continue the joust despite the blow, Schmeling was unable to get his legs to respond to the call." For the accidental knockout, Lust was awarded a disqualification.

A few weeks later, likely the same reporter added an episode to Ripley's "Believe It Or Not" after a hockey match between the local Tigers and the Drumheller Miners. While the Drumheller goalie cooled his heels in the "hoosegow," the Tigers failed to score on the open net for five exasperating minutes. Climaxing the "spasm," Drumheller streaked in on the Tigers and calmly deposited the puck behind net custodian "Moose" Bannan.

In a basketball match three weeks later, the Calgary Sharpshooters handed the Hat Terriers the thrashing of their lives, 65–26. "Feeling the equivalent of two cents worth of dog biscuits," the *News* reported, "the local Terriers returned to Medicine Hat under cover of darkness from Calgary after absorbing what is thought to be one of the worst defeats in provincial senior basketball history."

In losing times "The Office Cat" columnist of the city paper regularly birthed acidic aphorisms:

Blessed are the poor. They can act natural without fear of what people will think.

Cheer up, if you had things to do over again, you'd probably do them worse.

Man is the only animal we know of that can be skinned more than once.

The nice thing about the recent depression was that it included practically everybody.

Still it seems a shame to get rid of the unfit when all they need is some kind of a government job.

Many men who talk glibly of labor and capital never did the one nor had the other.

It takes a really great country to survive so many blunders.

It was all part of making do with what one had and making light of what one lacked. In 1935 a joke with several variants circulated the area. Two hobos were talking about the Depression.

"What would you do if you had all the money in the world right now?" the first asked.

"Well," said the other, "I reckon I'd pay it on my debts, far as it'd go."

ENCORE
"Everything's Popping!"

Medicine Hat proudly treasures Rudyard Kipling's legendary line as "the city with hell for a basement."* Lately the townspeople have become even prouder of something else they have discovered in their basement; water, in the shape of an underground gravel bed capable of producing 10 million gal. daily. With both cheap gas and water on tap, Medicine Hat envisions a future for itself as a sort of pocket Pittsburgh on the prairies. . . .

Time Magazine, *September 19, 1960*

Despite its dark chortling, the Depression cast a spell over Medicine Hat, an aura bleak and glum, lethargic and lasting, eons from that of the boom. One of the first to awaken was Alderman S. F. Scott, member of the Alberta Industrial Development Board. "It is hard to realize," he said in early 1947, "that we have been standing still for the best part of 30 years."

In dead of winter, 1950, the chamber of commerce held a strange conclave. Its paradoxical purpose was to discuss the ills of the city. From the likes of Bob Buss, Harold Purchase, Nelson Gahn, and others, rolled abuse after abuse—the

---

* *Redcliff patriots claim Kipling referred to their basement.*

inefficiences, the drabness, the inhospitableness. Said Buss, it all came down to the two "leths"—Lethbridge and lethargy, the first a model of progress and the second, the sickness of Hatters.

The critique recalled earlier complaints. In fact, the resemblance of the future to the past was uncanny. As at the robust turn of the century, the burg sat on the edge of a boom—followed by a lull, ecstacy, and then despondency.

Tentatively, new industries approached—first the Northwest Nitrochemicals in 1955 and then the Goodyear Tire and Rubber Company in 1959, the former benefitting from a fixed assessment for fifteen years and the latter from an aquifer, an underground river, pure and cool.

Even the parched land at last found moisture through the St. Mary's Irrigation Project. As agriculture slowly stabilized, the Hat backbone straightened. By 1951 the population finally exceeded that of 1913, and ten years later it topped 24,000.

"The city that used to have everything! *now has* everything plus!*" exclaimed a Medicine Hat Chamber of Commerce advertisement which offered prospective industries the services of geologists, architects, engineers, and business consultants "at no cost."*

Just when spirits lifted, the miniboom fizzled. Perhaps because irrigation benefits had limits and cheap power was everywhere, the sixties delivered little of their promise, and population growth was negligible.

The delay of prosperity invited an interlude of colour, spark, and lightness, rather like a comic short feature before the main event. None was better suited to orchestrate this preliminary than Harry Veiner. And he did it single-handedly.

A showboat, a hustler, a philanthropist, and mayor for twenty-one years, Veiner was a man of a thousand contests, with boundless self-confidence and unmitigated gall. He specialized in challenges—regional, national, and intercontinental. He bet he could beat a horse in a twenty-five yard race, a Scottish bigwig in booting a football, a Toronto mayor in a six-and-a-half mile walk, the Havana mayor in a sugar cane-cutting contest. He raced in toboggans and bathtubs, boxed professionals, and wrestled alligators. The more absurd the challenge, the more unqualified he was to compete, the better. And most often he won. Unhappily, despite drawing the initial industries of the fifties, and for reasons beyond his powers, Veiner never quite succeeded in turning the spotlight from himself to the city he certainly loved.

Another longstanding public servant, Mayor Ted Grimm, would take the helm for most of the next momentous cycles.

It was the world energy crisis which precipitated the great boom of 1975–81—that, and the eternal gas stores beneath the city. In 1973, 1,262 gas wells were drilled in the Hat zone, double those of 1971. Simultaneously, building permits soared from $889 thousand to $21 million. And in just eleven months of 1974, they totalled $125 million.

The next year the city built 571 new homes, breaking its 1913 record of 463; in 1976 it set the new mark of 648. Long its own developer, it ran out of lots, and when new ones were offered, people queued up at 5 and 6 AM to buy them. Adding to the old corporate entrepreneurs of the Yuills, the Sissons, and others, a new developer, Tom Sunderland, appeared, and though his relations with civic authorities were sometimes uneasy, the greater strain by far was that of the lightning expansion itself which so reshaped the city. From 26,000 in 1971, the population soared to 40,000 ten years later.

Hundreds of millions of dollars poured in, so much that one journal claimed the Hat was now making growth a way of life. Beneficiaries included a world-scale fertilizer complex, the petrochemical industries, and the new hospital, airport, sewage treatment plant, and the Medicine Hat Mall.

So many firms had entered the new Eden by late 1981 that the chamber of commerce staged a welcoming party for the new corporate collage. City fathers prided themselves in the fact that even with the pellmell expansion, tax and utility costs for an average 1,050-square-foot home on a 50-foot lot were only $751.53 in 1979, the lowest by far of Alberta cities. Particularly pleasing was the fact that Lethbridge, the sometime object of envy, was a distant second at $1,219.84.

Like gas bubbling from the riverbed, enthusiasm seeped everywhere. The chamber of commerce resurrected the pronouncement of Walter Gordon, chairman of the Royal Commission on Canada's Economic Prospects, that

Alberta would be the manufacturing centre of North America by century-end. "He is going to be right," effused chamber manager Vaughn Hullock. "We've got everything they need—water, coal, oil, gas."

As in 1912, delight and *joie de vivre* triumphed. Ray Switzer, area supervisor of the Energy Resources Conservation Board, broadcasted, "Everything's popping!" Eyeing the growing gas network, he deemed it security against any planetary disturbance. "This place is so tightly tied together by pipelines," he quipped, "an earthquake would never be felt."

Civic planners projected population growth into infinity—58,000 by 1990 and 103,000 by 2000. To avoid hourly annexations, they recommended a massive takeover of 3,375 acres from Improvement District 1.

Then the bubble burst. Oil, gas, and agricultural prices collapsed, drought again gripped drylanders, interest rates skyrocketed, and stocks, building starts, and land values plummetted. Foreclosures multiplied, and for the first time in history, banks, trust companies, and financial cooperatives in Alberta went under.

Compounding these evils, the National Energy Program introduced such catastrophic taxation that all enterprises dependent on cheap gas were shell-shocked. The greenhouse and petrochemical industries, especially, were sent reeling.

As usual, those caught in the fierce downdraft underestimated its power. Orville Wright, manager of the Hat Maple Leaf Mills, had no sooner remarked how stable flour milling was in a recession than the great mill, resident for seventy years and employer of ninety men, closed for good. And Dan Tassel, director of communications of Canadian Fertilizer Industries, had no sooner predicted a "rosy" future for fertilizer than a chief competitor, Western Co-operative Fertilizers, formerly Northwest Nitro-chemicals, the first of the new industries, terminated operations and partially dismantled.

As the population again stalled, some reflected on the fond hopes spawned by booms. Long before, at the height of the pre-Great War bonanza, one observer wrote, "The Hat expects to have a population of half a million by the time its young men are middle aged." Seventy-five years later, after these young men and half their sons and daughters were dead, it seemed clear that the day of the megalopolis was still distant. For those Hatters mindful of their own history and of the dislocations attending drastic change, however, it was probably just as well.

Here, where the South
Saskatchewan turns against
the great sandstone cliffs, the
Indians named it the Place of
the Medicine Hat.

Early townspeople belittled the native element, rejecting its claim to the land and downplaying its contribution in helping newcomers adjust to the frontier. "The redman is the only curse hanging over the prosperity and growth of the NorthWest Territories," grumbled *The Times* editor in April 1887. "That the government should allow them to run rife over the whole country when they could easily be restricted to a reservation, is an insult."

They called themselves the "pioneers." These men, gathered for this photograph years later, had been the first to settle in the valley in the summer and fall of 1882. The travelling Toronto *Globe* correspondent identified them as "cowboys, bull-punchers and speculators . . . an incongruous crew." Left to right: Bill Johnson, Robert Watson, J. H. G. Bray, George Connors, F. Wilton, Bob McCutcheon, and James Sanderson.

James Sanderson and his
Métis crews gathered
trainloads of buffalo bones
during the summer months of
the 1880s. By 1886 a few bison
could still be spotted on the
prairie, but by decade-end the
magnificent beasts had
vanished. The bones were
used to make bleaching,
fertilizer, and explosives.

Owning and operating a
"ranche" was a sure mark of
success among the young men
who were the first
entrepreneurs of Medicine
Hat. The resulting close
relationship between ranchers
and businessmen facilitated
the formation of the men's
Cypress Club in 1903.

First came the surveyors, then
the men building the grade.
Over 4,000 navvies laid the
steel as the transcontinental
railway made its way across
the prairies.

The City of Medicine Hat, all
clear for launching.
Steamboats provided a
valuable link in the early
1880s between the coal fields
at Coalbanks (now
Lethbridge) and the CPR
divisional headquarters at the
Hat. After the stage-coach era,
a passenger service began in
January 1899 on the newly
completed Crowsnest Railway
line to Lethbridge.

Above: **The first brickyard in Medicine Hat was opened by a Mr. Corbin in 1886. The following year Ben McCord opened another. Jacob Purmal, whose brick operation is pictured here, produced his first bricks in June 1896. His plant was a predecessor of IXL industries.**

Facing Page: **American by birth, Nigger Molly settled first at Fort Walsh in the 1870s. Some admired her and employed her as a domestic; others despised her as the embodiment of frontier evil. "Nigger Mollie was a large woman . . . and she wore a bustle," wrote W. H. McKay, scion of the prominent half-breed McKay clan, and early resident. "But it wasn't an** ordinary one, but one that was made to order out of well tanned buffalo hide. It had six compartments, each large enough to hold a short quart bottle of whiskey. She also had a brassiere made out of the same material, capable of holding two quart bottles."

A group of young railwaymen, calling themselves the "Colombian Minstrels" and later the "Georgia Minstrels," donned their costumes, blackened their faces and hands, and took to the stage to perform the music and dances, skits and antics of the American black vaudeville tradition. A highlight of the show was a unique strut, the "regular down south darky cake walk."

A host of masculine admirers and hockey enthusiasts clamoured for admittance at the doors of the rink but they were refused entrance to the ladies' hockey matches. Later, however, they were permitted to view this picture.

36

Facing page: **J. K. Drinnan arrived in 1885, as a teacher. In March 1889 he left the principalship of the school to publish the Medicine Hat** *Times.* **Within five years the paper was enmeshed in a fatal struggle with the CPR interests of the community.**

Above: **The bane of women of early Medicine Hat—the dirt and dust. Come summer, without fail, the townspeople began to ask the familiar question: "When will the water wagon (above) sprinkle the streets?"**

ORANGEMAN PROCESSION MEDICINE HAT JULY 13 1908

Above: **Every July 12th was an exciting day in Medicine Hat. The parade of the Orangemen, with Prince William leading the faithful on his white horse, and the Citizens' Band, led by stalwart *Catholic* Michael Leonard providing the beat, brought hundreds of townspeople onto the streets.**

Facing page: **John Niblock was thirty-eight years old when he assumed the superintendency of the Medicine Hat Division of the Canadian Pacific Railway in 1887. He supplied the CPR cabooses with the following verse: "It chills my blood to hear the blest Supreme / Appealed to lightly on each trifling theme. / Maintain your manhood, profanity despise, / To swear is neither brave, polite nor wise." He ran the railway, and some claimed the community itself, with an iron fist. When he was transferred from Medicine Hat in 1899, he left a substantial railroad town.**

The Citizens' Band was
organized in 1893. Michael
Leonard, the town's first
baker, nurtured the band in
its earliest years. An Irishman
who loved melody, Leonard
and his son, Joseph, provided
much of the push to keep
music foremost in the rough,
pioneering years.

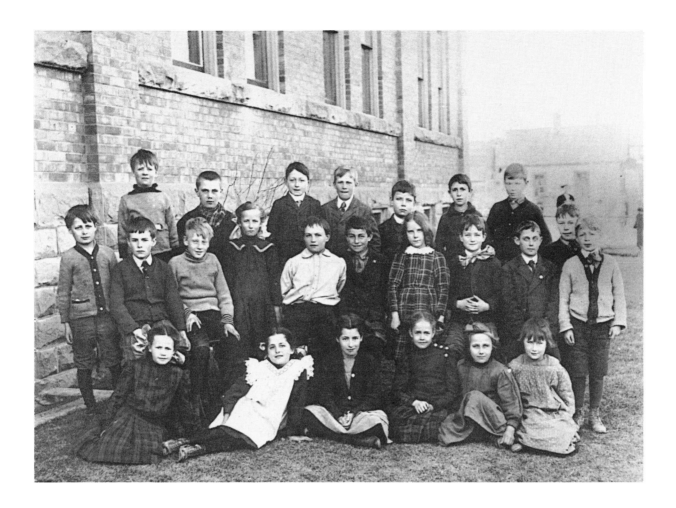

"You are afflicted here . . . by too much freedom on the streets at night and habits are acquired there altogether incompatible with discipline and progress at school," said a school inspector in the Territorial period. "Few teachers, very few teachers, can maintain order in your school."

While we were [in Medicine Hat] we heard accounts of rattlesnakes and other large reptiles being found and I asked the teacher if it were possible for one of his boys to get me a live rattlesnake and he said he thought there was no doubt but what they could and he would see what he could do in the matter. Less than an hour after I had spoken to him, two boys came down the street to where I was and one of them had a rattlesnake and the other also had a large snake which was called a bullsnake. Each boy had a string round the neck of the snake and just trailed it along behind him all along the road.

John Macoun, Autobiography, 1893–94

Above: **The first hospital in the North-West Territories, a dream realized by CPR Superintendent Niblock, was opened in 1889. So grateful was Niblock for the community support, that it brought him, he said, nearly to tears.**

Facing page: **William Cousins, centre, arrived in the Valley of the South Saskatchewan in May 1883. A youthful twenty-seven years of age, he remained in town and became perhaps its most distinguished citizen. Early owner of *The Times,* he served as city mayor and sparkplug with the agricultural society, the masons, and board of trade. Repeatedly bombarded by**

American reports that Medicine Hat was the home of the blizzard, he joked in old age, "If you registered at a hotel in Chicago and stated your residence to be Medicine Hat, they gave you an outside room so you could get cooled off."

The Assiniboia Hotel, under construction here, was the pride of Captain Horatio H. Ross, early entrepreneur and steamship skipper, who also schemed to develop a resort on Galt Island, down river. Opened in December 1898, it was the finest facility of its kind on the prairies, with steam heat, acetylene gas lighting, and an adjoining bowling alley. It was destroyed by fire on December 2, 1945, and rebuilt across the street.

From the outset it was clear that the fundamental shortage in the surrounding "empire" was water. Here the A. P. Phillips crew drill a 3,200-foot well. At the bottom of many holes was the deadly damp gas which claimed several early settlers.

Upon seeing the CPR gardens at
the Medicine Hat railway depot
in June 1892, Rudyard Kipling
noted ". . . a painfully formal
public garden with pebble paths
and foot-high fur trees . . . and
not ten yards from the track a
cinnamon bear and a young
grizzly standing up with
extended arms begging for food.
It was strange and beyond
anything that this bold telling
can suggest."

A panorama of Medicine Hat from north of the river, in the lull before the boom, 1906.

While almost every city and town in the West has been either on its knees to the transportation kings, or shaking its fist in their faces, imploring or threatening, calling meetings and passing empty resolutions, and so on, there is one town which has simply snapped a finger and thumb at them, and gone on its way rejoicing. This statue of independence, standing on the banks of the Saskatchewan, is "The Hat," and its independent spirit is born of mother earth in the form of natural gas. They have no coal bills, no coal scuttles, and no smoke and no ashes and they do not have a couple of inches of black dust on the sidewalk before each house, and the 'wimmen' folks do not have the mark of Cain across their faces every meal time.

J. M. Bain, Winnipeg Free Press, *February 18, 1907, during the fuel famine.*

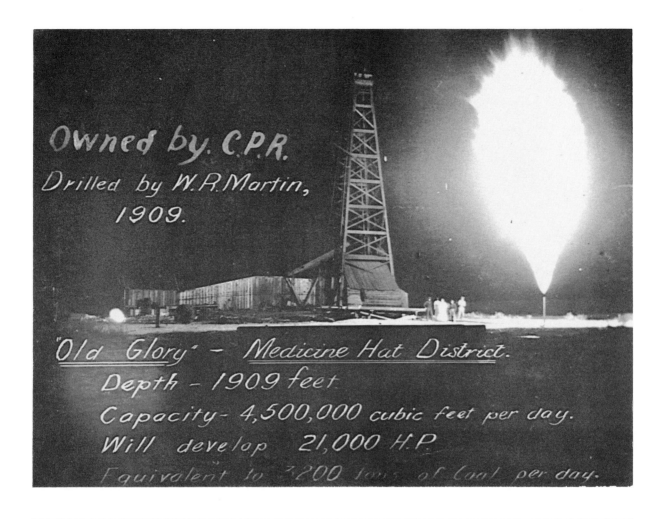

Owned by. C.P.R.
Drilled by W.R.Martin,
1909.

"Old Glory" — Medicine Hat District.
Depth — 1909 feet
Capacity— 4,500,000 cubic feet per day.
Will develop 21,000 H.P.
Equivalent to 3200 tons of Coal per day.

Blowing off gas wells by ignition was a tourist attraction for years. "Shooting a flame into the air like a fiery geyser with a deafening roar that outdoes Niagara, making the air vibrate and seeming to make the earth tremble," said one description, "is a sight which is never forgotten."

The new order and the old—
the industrial colossus of the
Alberta Clay Products, and
two blanket-clad Indian
women on the tracks, 1912 c.

The railway and its people
were always a central part of
the Hat life. Someone once
commented that if the railroad
ever re-routed its main line,
Medicine Hat would have to
fold up and leave.

Lake of the Woods Mill, 1913
c., one of three great new
flour mills, founded on the
expectation that the Hat
environs would be the coming
granary of the world.

From early days, Elkwater
Lake in the Cypress Hills, a
strange prominence untouched
by the last glaciation, was the
campground for Hatters
willing to brave bad roads.
"Old Baldy" hill is in the
background.

A lazy day in the shade of a
copse along the South
Saskatchewan River.

A butcher's display and a
Christmas worth celebrating at
the peak of the boom, 1912.

Land boomers in the
Hollinger Real Estate Office in
the frenzy of 1912. Established
in 1907 by Curtis Hollinger
who foresaw the future, this
agency was one of nearly a
score that worked night and
day during the land rush.

The construction crescendo
included these new homes on
the north side of 4th Street,
S.E., then Upper Montreal
Street. Many were still
occupied seventy-five years
later.

Amid the expansion, local contractor J. E. Lussier built many prominent buildings in the city, such as the Dominion Grocers Limited Wholesale block seen here, October 1913. The building still stands on North Railway Street.

Facing page: **In the glorious homesteading year of 1911, Ginther alone sold 10,000 acres of farmland in the dry belt. His real estate network stretched halfway across the globe.**

Above: **Agricultural displays touted the region as a horn of plenty. This show of vegetables, cut flowers, and house plants in the Nordeau Hall included a table of produce from the Ronalane Irrigated Farm. Unlike dryland promotion, irrigation advertisements often mentioned the unmentionable —drought.**

For several years the Sons of England (along with several chapters of the International Order of the Daughters of the Empire) represented the strong British element in Medicine Hat. This prize-winning horse-drawn float depicted a Man O' War in the Dominion Day Parade, 1912.

Cricket, New Year's Day 1913,
at the ball park below
Crescent Heights. Pictures like
this were used to attract
Britishers into the Hat haven.

From earliest days, foot racing
was a most important sport in
Medicine Hat. It was not so
much the one-hundred-yard
dash, or in this case the six-
mile marathon, that attracted
the attention, as the wagering.
With every race, lucre changed
hands freely, for the Hat was
not only a sporting town but
a betting town.

The Dreamland Theatre, here featuring "The Squaw's Revenge," brought locals the best of the silent flicks. It had 350 seats and a five-piece orchestra. For years movies were the highlight of youthful lives in the Hat.

Saturday morning was showtime in Medicine Hat and we took our places in the front row at the Roxy or Monarch Theatres with astonishing regularity, having paid the 10 cents admission charge and having loaded up at Sarge's Confectionery with jawbreakers, licorice and bubblegum. The afternoons were invariably spent duplicating the daring escapades witnessed that morning with the usual argument as to who would be the head honcho, a cowboy or an Indian.

Russell A. Dixon, "The Hat, The Creek and the Hills," 1980.

Young girls sunning on the walkway of Riverside Park, 1912 c. From the beginning, parks figured prominently in city plans to create an oasis in the aridity.

Alex Wallace, typesetter in *The Times* office. During the settlement period, William Cousins sparked the resurgence of *The Times* after its temporary demise in the 1890s, as a Conservative foil to the Liberal *News*. By 1913 the *Medicine Hat Call* became the third, though shortlived, newspaper.

Fire, the nemesis of wooden
towns, 1911. This
conflagration at the site of the
present Assiniboia Hotel
destroyed three stores,
including that of William
Cousins.

For decades the centre of
communications and travel
and the only link to the
outside was the railway.
During the boom, city fathers
expected numerous new rail
lines almost hourly.

By 1913 an air of stately
substance pervaded the city—
Second Street from City Hall,
looking east.

The great moment north of
Redcliff—turning the sod on
the ill-fated Hanna–Hat rail
line. Board of Trade President
Lorne Laidlaw with shovel
and Mayor Brown to the right,
1914.

Facing page: **Col. Nelson Spencer, longtime public servant of the Hat, helmsman in the boomtime, and bitter foe of Archie Hawthorne in the fiercely contested 1915 election following the bust.**

Above: **Laying the cornerstone of the Connaught School, October 1912. The school opened the next year with twelve teachers serving grades 1–8. It sat literally in the country, with a big slough to the north which the children regularly waded through. In the retrenchment after the boom, critics complained that the school was one more example of a facility meant for** a metropolis triple the size of Medicine Hat.

Facing page: **Archie Hawthorne, former Territorial cycling champion, and mayor during the difficult years of cutbacks in 1915 and 1916.**

Above: **Calves drinking from a public fountain on Kingsway. Many scenes in the stagnation after 1913 recalled earlier, "less civilized" times.**

Facing page: **St. Patrick's Catholic Cathedral, seen here about 1918, was built in 1912 to accommodate five to ten times the congregation resident from 1915–45. Neo-Gothic in style, it had a copper roof, solid oak doors, and round rose windows imported from France.**

Above: **The Redcliff Knitting Factory after the tornado, 1915. The wind funnel tore the roof off the Laurel Hotel, the Ornamental Iron Factory, the Redcliff Clay Products, and completely wrecked the two-storey, solid brick Redcliff Planing Mills. Elliot and Lang's icehouse was cut in two with part blown one way and part the other.**

THE ALBERTA LINSEED OIL MILLS, LIMITED.

With the economic
downswing, Hatters
experienced many evils,
including disastrous fires.
Unlike several other industries
which closed between 1914
and 1916, the Linseed Oil
Mills recommenced operations
in the same location and
lasted another seventy years.

The Medicine Hat Crayon
Company, one of a spate of
business casualties by late
1915. Gradually the buildings
in the river valley area
disappeared and were
replaced by light industries.

Recruits for Armageddon lined up near the old baseball diamond on Riverside. As troops left for the front, banners pronounced, "We are on our way to Tipperary" and "We'll be back for Christmas."

The feast of the victors—ladies
serving a picnic lunch to
returning soldiers at Riverside
Park, 1919.

The end of the Great War
brought the Age of the
Automobile perceptibly closer.
Here new Fords and Ford
chassis are unloaded from
boxcars.

MAYOR BROWN
PLOUGHING. JAN. 23, 1919.
MEDICINE HAT, ALTA.

In the third year of an interminable drought, Mayor Brown, in the height of absurdity and false promotion, went ploughing in midwinter, 1919. Two years on, the United Agricultural Association of Medicine Hat commandeered a "rainmaker" who promptly sustained the drought and delivered another crop disaster. By 1926 the huge agrarian hinterland westward was 80 percent permanently abandoned.

"It is sufficient to say," revealed a chamber of commerce brief in 1939, "that in the Medicine Hat area without irrigation there is a picture of bleak desolation, of abandoned farms, of families living in poverty, and of huge sums being expended in unproductive relief, without any possibility of repayment. The morale of the people in these drouth areas is being destroyed."

MEDICINE HAT GOLF CLUB
JAN., 25, 1919.

By the time of this winter gathering of golfers in January 1919, the links in the city had been in place for two decades. In the interwar period at Medicine Hat, a joke circulated about a Scottish golfer who had not played for many years. When asked why, he said, "Because I lost my ball."

Before this action about 1920,
Medicine Hat teams had won
pennants in the Alberta
Professional Baseball League
and the Western Canada
League.

The Medicine Hat Swimming Pool beyond Fifth Avenue United Church was one of several swimming holes, always popular because of the intense summer heat, 1925 c.

In late March, with winter hardly gone, the cry around the school was, "Coming down to the Ogilvies after school?" The swimming season had started and almost daily for a few weeks we would be in and out of the concrete pools where the boiler water was expelled for re-circulation; swimming cozily in 80-degree water and climbing out into 45-degree air.

With the warmer weather in May the aquatic activities shifted to Strathcona Island, a long crescent of wild, sandy land, covered with small elm and poplar scrub. We congregated where the high water of the Saskatchewan cascaded over a huge concrete conduit stretching from the mainland to the island. The fact that a sewer emptied a quarter mile upstream and that we often had to submerge to avoid floating fragments of raw sewage gave little concern. Our parents raised no outcry and, strangely enough, I cannot remember anyone contracting any ailment.

By late June the watercourse became nearly dry and we would retreat to the "Scouts," a swimming hole beneath a high tree-shaded bank behind Strathcona Island and when that pool shrank to waist depth in midsummer it was off to the north side of the main river at the end of the traffic bridge.

William Temple, Medicine Hat News, *June 14, 1971.*

85

In the late teens and early twenties, lavish productions were assembled to titillate the local fancy and display the exotic arts. Above is an actress in "The Sand Toy," a play performed by the Medicine Hat Operatic Company at the Empress Theatre, December 12, 1919. This coy individual study captured the delight and charm the plays held for the thespians themselves.

One aspect of the flourish of
culture between the wars—the
Medicine Hat Philharmonic at
its production of "Elijah," Fifth
Avenue Church, Christmas
1921.

At one time or another, it
seemed that Medicine Hat
manufactured everything—
including this short-lived line
of gramophones, 1922 c.

The Parade of Progress in 1923
celebrated the fortieth
anniversary of the burg.
Ironically, it was held amid a
general downturn and the
extermination of the dry belt
farmer, and following the year
in which there were the
fewest new building starts in
the city's recorded history.

Railwaymen and their ladies
at the silver anniversary banquet
of the Brotherhood of Locomotive Engineers, 1923. The
influence of railway unions
extended back many years in the
rail town. The first railway "ball,"
sponsored by the Brotherhood
of Locomotive Firemen and
Railway Brakemen was held
in December 1889 and featured
the parents of several seen
here.

The interior of the fashionable
New Club Cafe on the eve of
the Great Depression.

In early morning, June 10, 1935, a long freight train, boxcars swarming with two thousand malcontents bound for Ottawa, pulled into the CPR yards at Medicine Hat. They remained for twenty-four hours. The community responded by feeding them, challenging them to a baseball match, joining them at a large public rally in the evening, and lending them the arena in which to spend the night. The trek ended in riot at Regina on Dominion Day.

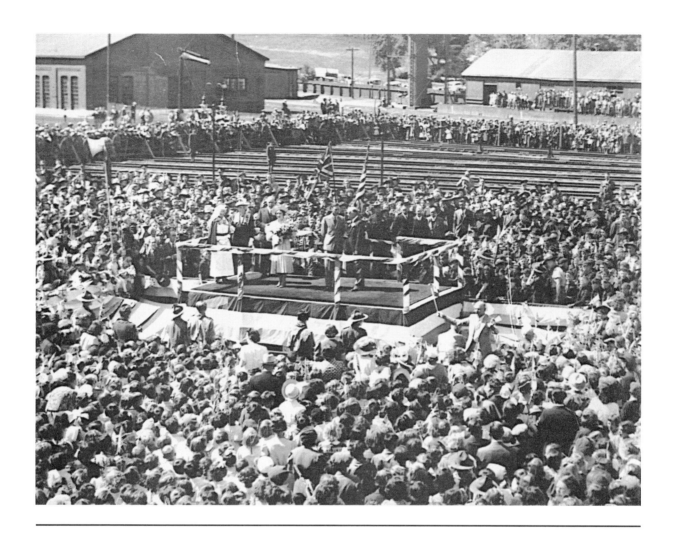

The memorable visit of King
George VI and Queen
Elizabeth, 1939. The whole
city and half the surrounding
territories witnessed the
spectacle.

The Crystal Ice Company cutting blocks from its river field for refrigeration, 1914 c. George Bean is seen here working the ice with a pike pole. It was then "spudded," or broken into smaller pieces, and then pulled by a team of horses up an incline onto a "bench," or platform, from which it was transferred to a sleigh and hauled to the icehouse. With artificial refrigeration, the practice gradually disappeared in the 1940s and 1950s.

This aerial view depicts the Hat about 1940. It extends from the CPR yards and roundhouse, west to Fifth Avenue, east to Ninth, and north to the still sparsely built-up Riverside subdivision centred by St. Patrick's Cathedral.

Facing page: **High jinks during a break near the brewery, along the banks of Seven Persons Creek.**

Above: **Making shells at the Alberta Foundry and Machine Shop, WW 11. During the conflict the foundry was completely turned over to war production and manufactured hundreds of thousands of anti-aircraft and shrapnel shells. Originally its chief investors were H. C. Yuill, one of the most successful capitalists in the city, and J. E. Davies, the first manager.**

Over more than seven decades of operation, it specialized in castings, forgings, valves, and even fire hydrants.

Facing page: **In the 1950s the Medicine Hat Police moved from the basement of city hall to the armouries on First Street, site of the present-day health office. The police occupied this building until 1965 when they moved to their present location on Ash Avenue. A long-serving lawman of the community was James Cairney, opposite.**

Above: **The opening of Service Flight Training School #34 in Medicine Hat in 1940 was a boon to the community after the Depression. Construction of the aerodrome began with the removal of the old stampede and exhibition buildings on the site of the present airport. Every nine weeks the school trained sixty new pilots. Several young English pilot-instructors fell in love with local girls and returned after the war to make their homes. This photograph shows the mess hall at the training school.**

Long touted as the salvation of Medicine Hat area agriculture, irrigation, even the "Big Wheel System," had its bedevilments.

Many agricultural agents advertize that they are prepared to show returned soldiers how to make a success of farming. . . . May we hope that as soon as the military rules of secrecy can be relaxed, this information will be released also to farmers.

"City Glances," Medicine Hat News, *August 10, 1945.*

Hatters appeared as Arabs, begging for water, in this sardonic publicity stunt at the inauguration of the St. Mary's Irrigation Scheme, 1951.

At a memorable moment, Sheik El Hamid Buss of the El Hamid Oasis, Medicine Hat Desert . . . addressed federal Agriculture Minister James G. Gardiner, known as "Man of Many Pockets": "Oh Man of Many Pockets, it is written by the prophets that in this, the year of no summer, we who live in the great and arid desert of Medicine Hat, shall leave our domiciles, and shall make voyage to this place of much water. In our land, the only water we have is dropped by utter accident from a cloud that passes by, bound for another destination. In this, the year of no summer, we have had many such accidents, and much water has fallen, praise Allah, upon the lands of our people. . . . In any normal year, by the beards of the prophets, the only water that we can be sure about, is the water content in our tears, as year after year, we watched our crops wither and die. We make this pilgrimage to seek this favor of you, that this water that is gathered by the St. Mary's may be shared by our people. . . . Oh Man of Many Pockets, we take our leave now, with hope in our hearts, joy in our bosoms, and happy memory of this day of days. We would ask that you take to the great Sheik at Ottawa word that when election day comes again, our tribesmen will go to the polls, and if your work carries on, you will not go to the cleaners."

Medicine Hat Chamber of Commerce papers, M86.9 f6110

For at least eighty years,
Medicine Hat greenhouses
have supplied roses and cut
flowers for the Prairies. By the
1950s, twenty-eight acres were
under glass. This 1952 photo
shows how roses packed in
newspapers are sprayed to
keep them fresh in transit.

Following the dry belt
catastrophe in the 1920s and
1930s, ranching resumed its
old importance. Here sheep
and cattle from the Murray
Ranch cross the river ice to
summer range, March 1955.

West of the Hat, sheep ranching
was a way out of the dry belt
disaster after the Great War.
Thriving on thistle and sage and
highly resistant to cold, able
to paw through snow for forage
and yielding meat and wool,
sheep, some believed, were the
natural animal for the aridity. In
the decades after this photo
in 1955, weak wool prices and
poor mutton demand greatly
diminished the flocks.

This late 1950s aerial offers a
view of the sparsely settled
South-West Hill subdivision
in the foreground, a mature
Riverside, and the new
suburb of Crescent Heights,
north of the river, with St.
Theresa's Academy gracing the
brow of the hillside.

Facing page: **Police Point Park, sometime lovers' lane and hooligans' hideout, viewed from Strathcona Island. Amid problems of revellers, spoilers, and litterers in the midseventies, a sign was posted in this wilderness park—"Let no one say, and say it to your shame, that all was beauty here until you came."**

Above: **Mayor Veiner of the Hat, left, and Mayor L. H. "Scoop" Lewry of Moose Jaw, digging in at a foot race, 1955 c. Veiner never missed a chance to advertise his city.**

Facing page: **Medalta Potteries opened in 1912 and operated till 1960. At one time the Potteries supplied the railways and major Canadian hotels with their dinnerware. In the Second World War Medalta produced dinnerware for the Allied messes. At its peak the company employed 350 people, half of whom were women. In the 1980s the "Friends of Medalta," a strong** community lobby, tried to have Medalta restored as a tourist and educational resource.

Above: **The Goodycar Tire and Rubber Company was the first major consumer of Medicine Hat's enormous underground water reserves discovered in the fifties. This sod-turning in 1959, many hoped, would mark the start of a new** industrial era. By the end of the sixties, Goodyear was importing seven million pounds of synthetic rubber from Sarnia, Ontario, five million pounds of carbon black from Hamilton and the U.S., and five million pounds of natural rubber from the Far East. Managed by the inaptly named Dick Skidmore, the plant produced 50,000 tires monthly.

Television had a remarkable
effect on a hub so long
isolated. Here school children
enjoy "Fun Time with Uncle
Bernie" in the early 1960s.

Controversy raged throughout
the community in 1961 with
the decision to raze the
impressive post office block
which had been opened in
1906. The spot is now
occupied by the Bank of
Montreal building.

Facing page: **The construction of the overpass on Allowance Avenue in 1962 helped solve the age-old problem of a city which grew up on both sides of the dangerous CPR yards.**

Above: **Through thick and thin, and widespread losses in the worst of times, ranchers have endured in the Hat region. Pictured here is the cattle ring of the Medicine Hat Feeding Company located in the Flats district of the city, on the site of the old Preston Planing Mill. Owned by the Taylor family, the business has been in this location for years. In the early 1950s the cattle feeding enterprise was expanded to include livestock auctions.**

The opening ceremonies on
October 3, 1971, of the campus
of Medicine Hat College. The
college began in the north
wing of the Medicine Hat
High School in 1965. The
attractive "cottage system"
facility, finished in brick from
the Medicine Hat Brick and
Tile Company, was located on
gently rolling prairie
bordering on Seven Persons
Coulee.

By the late 1970s the new heavy industrial core was well established at Brier Park. Shown here is the Goodyear plant, foreground; Western Co-operative Fertilizers (now closed), above; with Alberta Gas Chemicals further above and slightly to the left, and Canadian Fertilizers to the right. Generally the petrochemical industries used the natural gas in an ingenious new way—by breaking down its molecules to form desired compounds. Cancarb's production of carbon black was used as a strengthening element in tires, plastics, and heat deflector shields on rockets.

Photo Credits

MHMAGA = Medicine Hat Museum and Art Gallery Archives
GA = Glenbow Archives
PAA = Provincial Archives of Alberta

25	PC328.319 MHMAGA	56	PC328.169 MHMAGA	86	Gayner Collection, MHMAGA
26	PC2.12 MHMAGA	57	PC19.27 MHMAGA	87	FPC3594.2 MHMAGA
27	PC243.1 MHMAGA	58	M.75.21 MHMAGA	88	PC328.265 MHMAGA
28	PC62.9 MHMAGA	59	PC328.288 MHMAGA	89	PC328.126 MHMAGA
29	PC3520.26 MHMAGA	60	PC386.10 MHMAGA	90	PC3622.3 MHMAGA
30	PC235.1 MHMAGA	61	PC418.1 MHMAGA	91	PC218.4 MHMAGA
31	PC3509.2 MHMAGA	62	PC373.2 MHMAGA	92	PC223.11 MHMAGA
32	PC3521.72 MHMAGA	63	PC350.1.64 MHMAGA	93	PC713.1 MHMAGA
33	PC1725.1 MHMAGA	64	PC3518.25 MHMAGA	94	PC328.316 MHMAGA
34	PC196.1 MHMAGA	65	PC125.2 MHMAGA	95	PC3612.3 MHMAGA
35	PC174.3 MHMAGA	66	PC57.1 MHMAGA	96	Braun Collection, MHMAGA
36	PC2.10 MHMAGA	67	PC771.1 MHMAGA	97	PC40.10 MHMAGA
37	PC12.1 MHMAGA	68	PC328.149 MHMAGA	98	*Medicine Hat News* Photo
38	PC3545.6 MHMAGA	69	PC58.139 MHMAGA	99	PC3532.3 MHMAGA
39	PC180.24 MHMAGA	70	FPC55.926 MHMAGA	100	PC3595.10 MHMAGA
40	PC254.4 MHMAGA	71	NA 846-4 GA	101	PC218.16 MHMAGA
41	PC254.1 MHMAGA	72	PC9.1 MHMAGA	102	A8453 PAA
42	PC17.39 MHMAGA	73	PC3512.21 MHMAGA	103	PC88.26 MHMAGA
43	PC17.36 MHMAGA	74	NA 5002-6 GA	104	PC88.27 MHMAGA
44	PC61.13 MHMAGA	75	PC247.39 MHMAGA	105	PC328.137 MHMAGA
45	NA 3232-48 GA	76	PC206.15 MHMAGA	106	PC328.317 MHMAGA
46	PC17.4 MHMAGA	77	A5163 PAA	107	PC322.13 MHMAGA
47	PC328.131 MHMAGA	78	PC3517.12 MHMAGA	108	PC110.82 MHMAGA
48	NA 2159-20 GA	79	PC328.124 MHMAGA	109	*Medicine Hat News* photo
49	NA 4061-14 GA	80	PC104.4 MHMAGA	110	CHAT Television photo
50	PC318.119 MHMAGA	81	PC804.1 MHMAGA	111	PC110.57 MHMAGA
51	PC455.1 MHMAGA	82	PC137.7 MHMAGA	112	PC328.157 MHMAGA
52	PC318.106 MHMAGA	83	PC1756.1 MHMAGA	113	*Medicine Hat News* photo
53	PC318.110 MHMAGA	84	PC67.7 MHMAGA	114	*Medicine Hat News* photo
54	NA 2479-2 GA	85	PC110.39 MHMAGA	115	PC360.7 MHMAGA
55	PC135.46 MHMAGA				

Comment on Sources

The Provincial Archives in Edmonton hold many records regarding Medicine Hat and area. Most valuable are the papers of the following departments: Attorney-General (the sheriff's office and criminal case files), Municipal Affairs, Housing and Public Works, Recreation and Parks, and Education. Also useful are the files of the Water Resources Branch, the Board of Industrial Relations, the homestead records, Medalta Potteries, the Hat chapter of the IODE, and the Medicine Hat Agricultural Society.

Glenbow Archives hold the Medicine Hat *Times*, the *Medicine Hat Call*, *The Medicine Hat News* (pre-1940), numerous promotional pamphlets, and the informative papers of the Prairie Provinces Water Board, the Eastern Irrigation District, the Canada Land and Irrigation Company, the Special Areas Board, the CPR, Ross Ranches, Medalta Potteries, Bertram Souch, Fred Naab, W. L. Jacobson, Lawrence Burns, and J. H. G. Bray.

The Public Archives of Canada in Ottawa house a scattering of relevant documents, including promotional literature, agricultural fairs correspondence, and the records of the Department of the Interior.

In Medicine Hat, local council minutes and other records rest at City Hall. *The Medicine Hat News* recent vintage is at the College and also the News building. Several strong collections reside at the Medicine Hat Museum and Art Gallery Archives, including the chamber of commerce papers, the Cypress and Tilley East School Division records, the local industries collection, the F. M. Ginther papers, the hospital records, various ranch holdings, as well as interviews, clippings, newspapers, private manuscripts, local business papers, and the most outstanding photograph collection of the city.

Selected Readings

Carter, David J., *Behind Canadian Barbed Wire: Alien, Refugee and Prisoner of War Camps in Alberta* (Calgary: Tumbleweed Press, 1980).

Common, R., "Early Settlement About Medicine Hat, Alberta," *Geographical Bulletin,* 4:3 (1967): 25–43

Emson, J. B., *Dinosaurs to Defence: A Story of the Suffield Block* (London: Purnell Books, 1986).

Gershaw, F. W., "Highlights of Medicine Hat and District," (Medicine Hat: Modern Press, 1950?).

——, "Medicine Hat: Early Days in Southern Alberta," (Medicine Hat? 1950?).

——, "Ranching in Southern Alberta," (Medicine Hat: Modern Press, 1950?).

——, "Sidelights on Early Days in Medicine Hat and Vicinity," (n.p. 1950?).

——, "The Short Grass Area: A Brief History of Southern Alberta," (n.p. 1956?).

——, *Saamis: The Medicine Hat* (Medicine Hat: Val Marshall Printing, 1967).

Gould, Ed, *All Hell for a Basement* (Medicine Hat: City of Medicine Hat, 1981).

Hull, Raymond, ed., *Charles E. Shaw: Tales of a Pioneer Surveyor* (Don Mills: Longmans, 1970).

Jones, David C., *"We'll All Be Buried Down Here": The Prairie Dryland Disaster, 1917–1926* (Calgary: Alberta Historical Society, 1986).

——, *Empire of Dust: Settling and Abandoning the Prairie Dry Belt* (Edmonton: University of Alberta Press, 1987).

McKay, W. Henry, "The Story of Edward McKay," *Canadian Cattlemen,* 10:2 (September 1947): 76–77, 100–105.

——, "Early Days of Medicine Hat," *Canadian Cattlemen,* 12:2 (September 1949): 28–29, 32–33; 13:3 (March 1950): 48–49, 52–53; 14:7 (July 1951): 16–17, 20–21, 29.

Morrow, J. W., *Early History of the Medicine Hat Country* (Medicine Hat: *Medicine Hat News,* 1923).

Nelson, J. G., *The Last Refuge* (Montreal: Harvest House, 1973).

Wilson, L. J. Roy, "Children, Teachers, and Schools in Early Medicine Hat," *Alberta History,* 32:3 (Summer 1984): 15–21.

——, "Cultural Life in Medicine Hat, 1883–1905," *Alberta History,* 33:3 (Summer 1985): 1–8.

——, "Medicine Hat–The Sporting Town, 1883–1905," *Canadian Journal of the History of Sport,* 16:2 (December 1985): 15–32.

——, " 'Everlasting Squabble,' Medicine Hat in Crisis, 1891–98," *Alberta History,* 35:1 (Winter 1987): 1–12.

About the Authors

David Jones was born in Edmonton, Alberta, and educated at the Universities of Victoria and British Columbia. He is author or editor of several books on western Canadian history including *Midways, Judges, and Smooth-Tongued Fakirs* and his most recent, *Empire of Dust—Settling and Abandoning the Prairie Dry Belt*. His innumerable articles and reviews have appeared in such journals as the *Canadian Historical Review, Alberta History,* and the *Journal of Educational Thought*.

David is married with three children and currently teaches at the University of Calgary.

Born in Regina, Saskatchewan, Roy Wilson was educated at the Universities of Saskatchewan and Alberta and has been teaching for nearly thirty years. His interest in local history and education has led to the publication of articles and reviews in several periodicals including *Pedagogica Historica, Saskatchewan History,* and the *Saamis Review*.

Roy is an instructor in Canadian history and education at Medicine Hat College. He is married and has five children.

Donny White is the Curator of Cultural History at the Medicine Hat Museum and Art Gallery. Educated at the universities of Saskatchewan and Calgary, he is presently working on a graduate degree in museum studies from John F. Kennedy University in San Francisco.

Prior to his present employment Donny was program co-ordinator for the Fort Calgary Interpretive Centre and also a research officer for Saskatchewan's Provincial Historic Parks. He has been active in many organizations concerned with preserving western Canada's cultural heritage. His current interests include historic research on regional Indian and Metis populations and on ranching in the Cypress Hills.